Health, Hopes and Chances

A hopeless ignores chances

健康，希望和機會

灰者後機而靜

Sauce Huang

Order this book online at www.trafford.com
or email orders@trafford.com

Most Trafford titles are also available at major online book retailers.

Print information available on the last page.

ISBN: 978-1-4907-5847-3 (sc)
ISBN: 978-1-4907-5849-7 (hc)
ISBN: 978-1-4907-5848-0 (e)

Library of Congress Control Number: 2015905869

Trafford rev. 04/14/2015

 www.trafford.com

North America & international
toll-free: 1 888 232 4444 (USA & Canada)
fax: 812 355 4082

To Jo-En, Paul and Jay

給瓊英，伯彥和中彥

Contents
目錄

Preface: The Hopeless
序: 灰者

There are two kinds of hopeless people.
世間有兩種灰者。

The first kind is people who have no desire nor intention yet do not want to die.
第一種灰者是心灰意冷又不想死的人。

They may try Buddhism. No matter it is Mahayana or Theravada, they all believe in the theory relative to "emptiness". A true Buddhist is merciful, independent, self-controlled and peaceful.
他們可以信佛。不論是大乘佛或是小乘佛，都相信"空"的理論。真信佛的人慈悲為懷，自給自足；不礙他人，與世無爭。

However, people live on Buddhism do not believe the emptiness. They manage wealth or fame or both; like the managers of four mountains in Taiwan and ZhenFoZong.
然而，藉佛維生的人不相信空字。他們管名，管利或名利皆管；例如台灣四大名山和真佛宗的管事們。

The other kind of hopeless people lost their mind so that they are unable to live by themselves. They rely on others to survive.

第二種灰者是失心從而無法自力維生的人。他們完全依賴別人而生存。

Independence is to earn self's own living in the world. People who are able to be, but no plan for, independence; are either the lazy who just follow the nature or the junky who abandon themselves.

自立是在人間營生。能夠自立，而不打算自立，的人；是天生隨遇而安的懶者或後天自暴自棄的廢者。

Whoever hopes to, but impossible to be, independent; has the worst situation in the world. Since the second kind of hopeless people may not have hope, so that they may not feel sad; who definitively feel sad are relatives or friends of those hopeless people.

希望自立，而無法自力維生是人間最慘的事。但是，第二種灰者，也許沒有希望，所以他們也許不慘；肯定慘的是那些第二種灰者的親朋。

The hopeless ignore chances and keep quiet.

灰者後機而靜。

What the hopeless ignored are every single opportunity in their world so that they do not have any confuse which is "related to reality". Their minds are either quiet as of the first kind or unknown as of the second kind.

灰者們無視今日世界的任何機會；所以心中沒有"和現實相關"的紛擾。他們的心意不是第一種心如止水就是第二種心思莫測。

At least, judged from the appearance, their thoughts are independent to any "non-contact event" occurs now.

至少，表面上看起來，他們的心念對於現在發生的任何"非接觸事件"完全沒有反應。

My comment of "the hopeless ignore chances and keep quiet" is relative to: the wise move before chances, the smart change upon chances, the vulgar follow the changes and the stupid miss chances then if they aware of a chance later on, they regret about missing it.

相對於聖者先機而動，賢者見機而變，凡者隨機而行，愚者失機而悔；我的看法是，"灰者後機而靜"。

Whoever has dead mind does not keep any hope, they just keep on living; while whoever loses mind, are unable to show his/her hope and most of their hopes would die before the fulfillment. Chances do not mean anything to those two kinds of people.

心死的人，除了維生不抱任何希望；而失心的人，很難表達希望，那些希望大多胎死腹中。機會對這兩種人，沒有任何意義。

If you are not one of those two kinds of person, please watch for chances.

如果你不是這兩種人，請留意機會。

Sauce Huang
黃醬

3/31/2015
2015 年 3 月 31 日

Health, Hopes and Chances
A hopeless ignores chances

健康，希望和機會

灰者後機而靜

1. Love and Justice
私情與公義

People all care about love and justice.
What relative to love and justice are
personal benefits and public power.
沒有人不在乎情與義。和情與義相關的分別是
私利與公權。

In Chinese culture, Mozi promoted the real
justice via public benefits while Confucius
promoted the balance of love and justice.
Laozi analyzed the theory of love and justice
within the nature while HuiNeng pursued the
true love via personal power.
在中國文化裡頭，墨子講究的是公利的實義而孔子講
究的是情義的平衡。老子分析情義在自然裡頭的道理
而慧能追求私權的真情。

The Chinese teachings described above are all trying
to find eternal solution within the world and it is
quite the same in the Korean and Japanese cultures.
上述中國的各種教導都是在當世裡頭尋求永恆之道而韓國和
日本的文化也大致是這樣。

However, in Mid-Asia, Africa and Europe people pursue the eternity of staying with God after death while in India people pursue the eternity of escaping the transmigration of souls.

但是，中亞，非洲和歐美的文化追求死後與神同在的永恆而印度文化追求死後跳出輪迴的永恆。

The above two cultures expect eternity after death.
上述兩種文化都把永恆放在死後。

We know that the eternity has two sides; one is the unknown past and the other one is the unlimited future. Nobody clearly know either end of the eternity especially the unknown past.

我們知道永恆的概念包括兩端；一端是無知的亙古而另一端是無限的未來。這兩端，都沒有人清楚明白的知道；尤其是無知的亙古。

Because, the evidence of possible earlier human beings was the stone age Homo erectus only two million years ago. We are unable to communicate with other creatures yet; even if we can communicate otherwise, the earliest living creature was unicellular found in the fossil from four billion years ago. The simplest living creature, virus, seems rely on other living creatures to provide food, could it appear before unicellular?

因為，人類在地球上的遺跡好像是猿人模樣而猿人出現的時間也不過是兩百多萬年前可以玩石器的直立猿人。人類還沒有辦法和其他生物溝通；就算有辦法溝通，地球上的生物也不過是四十多億年前的單細胞生物可以留下化石。更簡單的病毒類有機體好像依賴生物的養分來複制，他們是否能夠比單細胞生物更早出現呢？

Even if virus could exist before unicellular we are unable to investigate any event in their history before four billion years ago and we do not know any event before that. Because as we know, virus only perform copying and mutation and based on the history we have recorded about virus since year 1899, we are unable to deduce any of their activities before unicellular existed.

就算在四十億年以前有類似病毒的簡單生命體，人類也查問不出他們在四十多億年以前的任何歷史事件，也就是，我們不知道更早以前的事件。因為現代的病毒只做複製和突變這兩個動作而在 1899 年以後人類所記錄的病毒歷史裡頭，無法推論病毒更早期的活動。

How about the history of matters? We do not clearly know how the earth started nor how the universe started. Hence, the unknown past is still waiting for the young generation to disclose.
無生物的歷史呢？我們不確實知道地球如何產生也不知道宇宙如何開始。所以，無知的亙古還有待年輕人去探索。

However, almost every culture dreams about eternity, hopes human beings do have unlimited future.
可是，幾乎每一個文化都嚮往永恆，都希望人類有無限的未來。

Since people will die, logically speaking, people should assign the hope of eternity after death.
因為人必定會死，所以在邏輯上，必須把永恆這個希望寄托在死後。

1-1. Chinese Culture
中國文化

But, Chinese culture seems do not care about this logic. Chinese people say "The furs stay after tigers die while the fames stay after people die." and "Keep my loyal heart to shine the history", both mean people should try to be a hero of the human society.
然而，中國文化似乎不顧這個邏輯。中國人說"虎死留皮，人死留名"和所謂"留取丹心照汗青"都建議人們在史書上留下英名。

They hope the history can pass down the name of heroes for million years. They refuse to think further. After accumulated too many, only a few names will remain.
他們希望藉著歷史去謀求世代相傳的萬萬世代的英名。他們卻不肯進一步想想。歷史越積越多，最後只有少數幾個名字能夠世代相傳。

In year 1911, they certainly did not know that the earth would be gone sooner or later. If at the time of the end of earth people had no other place to go then the eternity they expected would disappear forever. May be Chinese people did not really care about eternity.

在一百年前，他們當然不知道地球遲早會毀滅。如果在地球毀滅的時候，人類無處可去，那麼，他們期待的永恆就徹底落空了。也許中國人並不真正在乎永恆？

People still do not know where can they go when the earth die, with all the advanced technologies today. Hence, if they care about eternity, Chinese people should put eternity after death. I believe, Chinese culture only pursues million years of fames. It does not care about eternity; no matter the eternity of the past or for the future.

就算在今天，人類也還不知道地球毀滅的時候自己將何去何從。所以，如果在乎永恆，今日的中國人應該也把永恆放在死後才合情合理。我認為，中國文化只是追求有限的萬萬世代的英名。它確實不在乎永恆；不論是亙古還是未來的永恆。

1-2.　Reasonable Eternity
合乎邏輯的永恆

A culture of reasonable eternity should believe that a human soul will not die.
合乎邏輯的永恆文化必須相信人的靈魂不死。

There are two kinds of eternal soul. One is the soul of no birth nor death in Indian culture; a soul can change body between living creatures or escape the circling and stay in the paradise. The other one is the soul in the monotheism which once appeared would never die and the soul will live in the heaven or hell.
靈魂不滅又有兩種可能。一種是印度文化的不生不滅；靈魂可以在生物界輪迴而靈魂也可以脫離輪迴，常駐極樂世界。另一種是獨神文化的生而不滅，肉身死後，靈魂常住天堂或地獄。

Then, how does a soul be allowed to enter the heaven or the eternal paradise?
那麼，靈魂又如何上得天堂或極樂世界呢？

In a monotheism culture, the words
of God is the top guideline; while
in a reincarnation culture, there
are saints to teach their believers
how to behave.
在獨神文化，神的話至高無上；而在輪
迴文化，自有先哲指導信徒的言行。

1-3.　The words of God
神的話

The words of God are recorded in
different Scriptures, urge people to do
good things.
神的話記錄在各種經典裡頭，勸人為善。

However, the wisdom of people are always
limited and some mistakes will produce bad
result; so that a soul may go to heaven or
hell, at the judgement day or after death.
但是，人的智慧有限，難免做錯事，結惡果；所以在
審判日或死後，靈魂可以上天堂卻也可能下地獄。

The Torah of Judaism, the Old
Testament and New Testament of
Catholicism and Orthodoxy, the New
Testament of Protestantism, the
Quran of Islamism, the Book of
Mormon for Mormonism and the Most
Holy Book of Bahaism are some of
the words of God.

猶太教的摩西五經，天主教和東正教的舊約和新約聖
經，基督新教的新約聖經，伊斯蘭教的可蘭經，摩門
教的摩爾門經以及巴哈伊信仰的至聖之經都是神的話。

According to the words of God, in the Torah,
Jews are the choice of God; they believe they
are always the teacher of the whole human
beings. In the New Testament, there is a new
teacher of the whole human beings, Jesus; so
that the believers appreciate Jesus' mother,
Maria; but Catholicism accepts the logical
link of Trinity while Orthodoxy does not
accept it. An Orthodox insists that the Spirit
is from the Father only. Do the other hand, in
Protestantism, the believers look upon Jesus
as the only way to the heaven and they almost
ignore Maria.

根據神的話，在摩西五經裡頭，猶太人是神的選民；猶太人相信他們永遠是唯一的全人類導師。在新約中，出現了新的全人類導師，耶穌；因此教徒感謝耶穌的母親，瑪利亞；而且天主教徒接受了三位一體的邏輯連結，可是，東正教徒不同意，堅持聖靈只從天父而出。然而，在基督新教中，教徒們則強調耶穌是唯一的天堂之路，幾乎不再理會聖母。

However in Quran, Jesus is just one of Prophets, Mohammed is the last, the most important Prophet.
然而在可蘭經裡面，耶穌只是先知之一，穆罕默德才是最後，最重要的先知。

Besides above words of God, the Book of Mormon contains the history of Christianity in USA while the Most Holy Book and the Book of Certitude are the tool that Bahaism uses to unify all religions.
另外，摩爾門經包含美國的基督教歷史而巴哈伊信仰的至聖之經和篤信經則企圖一統所有的宗教。

So, there are quite a few versions of the
words of God.
所以，神的話有許多種版本。

1-4. The Teachings of Saints
先哲的指導

There are many religions in India,
nevertheless they all center at the soul
reincarnation and use the aging,
sickness and death as base of teachings
to encourage people doing good things.
在印度有多種宗教，但是它們都以靈魂輪迴為
中心，生老病死為教材勸人為善。

Most denominations of Hinduism suggest each
soul is part of the God, but due to the
complication of the world, when the soul lives
there it needs instructions from saints to
transform to a better group of living creature.
If that soul is lucky, it may escape the
cycling after death and stay in the western
paradise, do not have to see the sun of the
next day.

多數印度的教派主張每一個靈魂都是神的一部分，可是這個靈魂借住的世界太複雜所以靈魂在各種生物體借住的時候，需要先哲的指導，才能夠轉世到較好的族群裡頭。如果那個靈魂夠幸運，死後還可以跳脫輪迴，常留西方極樂世界，不必再看見明天的太陽。

Even Buddhism was created in India, it is more popular in other countries because the theory of "emptiness" is too hard to understand. The Buddhists only occupy a small percentage among religion people in India, about 1%.

由於"空"的概念非常不容易了解；所以，雖然無神的佛教誕生於印度，卻發達於國外。佛教在印度的信徒百分比不大，約佔百分之一左右。

Sikhism is different from other Indian denominations due to it does not discriminate caste nor gender addition to no idolatry. Among all religion believers Sikh occupies about 2% and Hindu occupies about 78%.

錫克教主張 "在種姓以及性別上不互相歧視"，加上不拜偶像，所以它不同於其他印度教。錫克教徒約佔印度信徒的百分之二左右，其他各種印度教教徒約佔印度信徒的百分之七十八左右。

If we count Buddhist and Sikh, the number of Gods in India can be many to none; but, every denomination in India believes the soul will live forever.

如果包括佛教和錫克教，印度教徒的神就從多神到無神；但是，每個在印度的教徒都相信自己帶有永生的靈魂。

Besides the native, there are about 14% of Moslems and 4% of Christians in India. 外來宗教，在印度，目前伊斯蘭教徒約佔百分之十四左右而基督教徒約佔百分之四左右。

1-5. Private Benefits & Public Power
私利與公權

In Chinese teachings from Mocius, Mencius, Confucius, Laozi to HuiNeng they all talked about private benefits and public power related to love and justice. The teachings taught people how to deal with different kinds of conflicts between love and justice.
在中國的教義，不論是墨子，孟子，孔子，老子還是慧能都是針對和情與義相關的私利與公權做研究。他們教導信徒如何處理情義的各種衝突。

The words of God and teachings
of saints must include the rules
of handling private benefits and
public power as well. That means
the prophets of God and teachers
of different cultures should
teach their people how to handle
the unavoidable conflicts
between love and justice, and
how to manage the private
benefits within public power.
神的話和先哲的教導也都必須包含處
理私利與公權的規則。也就是，神的
使者和各種文化導師必須教導各自的
信徒們如何處理必定會碰上的情與義
的矛盾，如何讓私利與公權並存。

2. War and Cooperation
戰爭與合作

The public power is to properly distribute private benefits. People hope that justice is able to untie the tangled node of love.

公權這個東西是用來適當分配私利的。人們希望，義可以解開情結。

People fight for love. In general, everyone fights for the love of the prospective spouse, a celebrity fights for the love of fans, a merchant fights for the love of customers, a politician fights for the love of voters; while ancient Chinese people fought for the love of the next generations. Ancient Chinese people cared about a good name after death so that they were fighting for the love of their following generations.

人們爭情。一般人爭伴侶的情，名人爭粉絲的情，商人爭客戶的情，政客爭公民的情；而古中國人，爭後代人的情。古中國人講究人死留名就是去爭後代人的"情"字。

Since there is a fight, a war is hence unpreventable. So, the longer people live, the more complicated their tangled nodes of love will be tied by the words of fight and war.

既然爭，難免戰。於是，人們日子過得越長久，他們的情結就被爭戰兩個字綁得越複雜。

When the members tied up by the node of love is more than two, there is politic issue. The key of politics is the public power.

當情結綁住的人數超過兩個，就出現政治。政治的關鍵就是公權。

Before the born of America, the public power was hold by the kings, and all the historical tyrants and fatuous kings did not have a nice ending.

在美國開國以前，世界上的公權大多掌握在國王手中，而歷史裡頭的暴君和昏君都無法善終。

The power of the king was formally reduced by the Magna Carta signed in year 1215. And it was until year 1689 when the Bill of Right set out the requirement for regular elections that the democracy started the first step.

國王的權力在 1215 年，自由大憲章簽署開始正式削減。到了 1689 年的權利法案規定，議員由合格公民自由選舉產生，民主才正式開步走。

Then, America was born in year 1776 and people of America finally abandoned the position of king and elected their leader, the president, directly.

然後等到 1776 年美國開國，美國人才廢除了國王的職位改成全民直選總統。

From 1776 to 1945, the only democratic countries were United Kingdom and United States. However in year 2015 most industrialized countries elect their legislators; even some countries of single party, like China, allows some representatives be elected.

由 1776 年到 1945 年，只有英美兩國維持民主政治。可是到了 2015 年在多數工業發達的國家，立法委員都是由公民投票選舉；甚至有些一黨專政的國家，包括中國，也給予人民一些區域代表的選舉權。

That means entering the 21st century people are holding the public power gradually. However the result of transferring public power from the king to the people did not necessarily benefit the people.
因此進入 21 世紀以後人民已經逐漸掌握了公權力。但是公權力由國王轉移到人民手中這件事，並不一定對人民有利。

2-1. The Shortcoming of Democracy
民主政治的缺點

Because of the waiting time for all voters to study the target problem, the vote will miss the best timing to solve the target problem; this is the natural defect of democracy.

因為投票表決需要等到大部分投票人明白問題，往往錯失解決問題的好機會；這是民主政治的先天缺點。

Secondly, regarding the making of laws, most legislators are not wise nor smart, so that they are unable to move before the chance comes nor to respond in time when the chance comes. The result is, the laws are always behind the needs of the real environment; this is the practical defect of democracy.

其次，在法律條款的制定上，多數立法委員不是聖賢，所以無法先機而動也無法見機而變。造成的結果就是，法律永遠落後於現實環境的需求；這是民主政治的實際缺點。

2-2. The Defects of Love
私情的毛病

There are natural and practical problems of love as well.
私情也有先天和實際的毛病。

First of all, as arranged by the nature, most women hope her husband is loyalty in love but most men search for talented beautiful women beyond love; that is why the porn business is growing more prosperous. This is the natural defect of love.
首先，天生人類，多數女人希望她的伴侶愛情專一可是多數男人卻喜歡越情尋求美色和才女；所以色情生意，越做越旺。這是人類私情上的先天毛病。

Secondly, most people love money. Almost everyone wish there are extra money at home, the more the better; however the resources of a society is limited, so that only a few families can be satisfied. This is the practical defect of love.

其次，絕大多數的人愛財。幾乎人人希望家有餘財，越多越好；然而社會的資源有限，所以只有少數家族得以如願。這是人類私情上的實際毛病。

2-3. The Duty of the Public Power
公權力的責任

The only duty of the public power is to fix the natural and practical defects of love properly.
公權力的責任只有一個，那就是它必須把私情的先天的和實際的毛病妥當修好。

As all eyes can see, the natural and practical defects of love have getting worse since the prevalence of democracy after year 1945. Entering the 21st century, the overflow of porn business and the serious inequality of wealth are global normality. That means in year 2015, the natural and practical defects of love are almost out of control.

自從 1945 年民主政治開始流竄全球以後，私情的先天毛病和實際毛病是有目共睹的越來越嚴重。進入 21 世紀，色情泛濫和嚴重的貧富不均，已經是全球的常態。也就是說，在 2015 年，私情的先天毛病和實際毛病幾乎已經完全失控了。

If we study it deeper, both defects of love are caused by fighting for limited objects. 究其原因，私情的兩個毛病都源於爭奪有限的東西。

Nice girls or loyal boys are rare, and the billionaires created by way more wealth are even less. Hence, to satisfy love, people must fight. Then, the public power should handle those fighting properly.
美好的女子或專情的男人很少，而更多的財富所造成的億萬富豪更少。所以，為了滿足私情，人們就必須爭奪。那麼，公權力就必須妥善處理那些爭奪。

The opposite side of fighting is cooperation. The public power must transform "some" amount of fighting force into cooperating force which is "big enough" to overturn the current trend before the defects of love is out of control.

爭奪的反面就是合作。公權力必須在私情的毛病絕對失控以前，把一部分"足夠扭轉局勢的爭奪力量"轉變成合作的力量。

Why does democracy fail to fix the natural defect and practical defect of love? Because, both of the natural defect and practical defect of democracy have no starting point for people to do some possible repairing jobs. Then, what were some different political ideas people adopted before year 1945 which can serve as references?

為什麼民主政治無法醫治私情的先天毛病和實際毛病？因為，民主政治的先天缺點和實際缺點根本無處著手去改善。那麼，在 1945 年以前，人類有過哪些不同的政治理念可以用來參考呢？

3. The Ball of LWJC
情爭義合球

In the following figure, the vertical
axis represents the seven degrees of the
strength of desire a person possesses
(half due to the born nature and half
due to the influences of environments),
from the states of war down to the state
of peace. The horizontal axis represents
how much the will lays on love or
justice. While the axis perpendicular to
the page represents how much goodness or
badness the result of an event shows, or
the result is not good and not bad so
that the event point is on the page.
在以下的圖解裡頭，縱軸代表一個人的慾望或強或弱
（半由天生，半因環境）；可以由爭到不爭，逐漸減
少，分成七個等級。橫軸代表一個人的心意有多麼注
重私情或公義。而垂直紙面的第三軸代表一個人參與
的事件結果，有幾分屬善或屬惡，或屬於無善惡之分
的紙面上。

You may recall major events of your life, think about each of them and find out where should you locate the event point within this ball of LWJC. The LWJC represents Love, War, Justice and Cooperation.

The Ball of LWJC

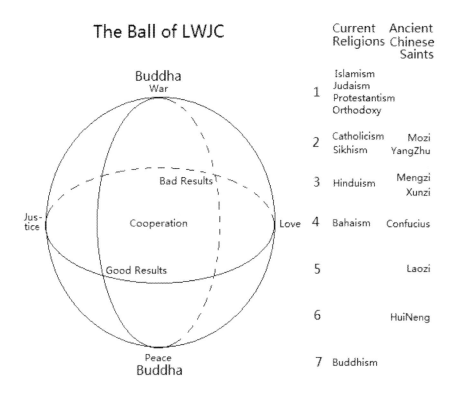

	Current Religions	Ancient Chinese Saints
1	Islamism Judaism Protestantism Orthodoxy	
2	Catholicism Sikhism	Mozi YangZhu
3	Hinduism	Mengzi Xunzi
4	Bahaism	Confucius
5		Laozi
6		HuiNeng
7	Buddhism	

您自己認為，到目前為止您一生中比較大的事件它們的事件點，都分佈在這個情爭義合球的哪一些部位呢？

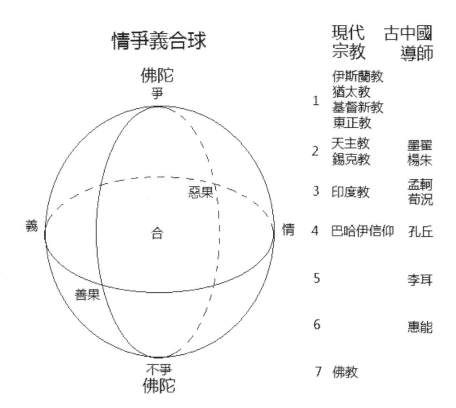

情爭義合球

佛陀
爭

惡果

義　　　　合　　　　情

善果

不爭
佛陀

	現代宗教	古中國導師
1	伊斯蘭教 猶太教 基督新教 東正教	
2	天主教 錫克教	墨翟 楊朱
3	印度教	孟軻 荀況
4	巴哈伊信仰	孔丘
5		李耳
6		惠能
7	佛教	

3-1. The Vigorous
積極份子

In ancient China, the small group of people who believed in Mozi or YangZhu were very vigorous; either die for justice (helping the vulnerable) or hunger for personal benefits (collecting all possible money). Those two kinds of people were lived more exciting than the followers of Mencius or Xunzi, in case of urgency, they did not care about their lives.

在古中國，相信墨翟或楊朱的那一小批人，生活得非常積極；不是為公義拼死救助弱小，就是為私利狠命大小通吃。那兩種信徒的日子都比孟子或荀子的信徒過得更加激動，必要時，他們可以將生死置之度外。

In the world today, Catholics establish hospitals and churches vigorously; preaching and healing; as strived as Mozi was doing in ancient China.

在今日世界，天主教積極開設醫院和教堂；一方面傳教，一方面醫人；和當年的墨子一樣努力。

Nevertheless, the earlier Catholics were not only vigorous but also so extreme to start wars. They started three wars in protecting the Holy City, Jerusalem. The first time in 1099, got it back; the second time in 1187, failed; the third time in 1228, got it back then lost it. Besides those, there were more than 10 crusaders wars started by Catholics.
但是，稍早的天主教不只積極，還蠻極端的發動戰爭。他們在聖地耶路撒冷保衛戰，發動過三次戰爭。第一次，1099 年奪回聖城；第二次，1187 年被奪後，反攻失敗；第三次，1228 年，奪回卻很快又失去。另外，以天主教為名的十字軍戰爭從 1096 年到 1291 年超過十次。

As of today, the ownership issue of Jerusalem still exists, however the Catholics quit already; Jews and Moslems are fighting over their holy city.
今天，耶路撒冷的問題還在，然而天主教已經置身事外；只剩猶太教和伊斯蘭教在爭奪他們的聖城。

Even though Catholics set the Jerusalem issue aside, they are very vigorous on fighting diseases. The vigorous occupy the second high level of desire in the ball of LWJC.

天主教教徒雖然不理聖城之爭，他們和疾病打仗還是做得非常積極。積極份子具有情爭義合球的第二高階慾望。

Catholics are not as extreme as Protestants.
天主教沒有基督新教教徒那麼極端。

3-2. The extreme
極端份子

Entering 21st century, besides some countries are having reasonable civil wars; on 2014-6-29 a multinational religion country was born and that Islamic State is creating wars.
進入 21 世紀，除了有些國家的內戰正在打著可以理解的仗；2014 年 6 月 29 日還出現了橫跨多國的宗教國家而那個伊斯蘭國正在製造戰爭。

When part of citizens are oppressed up to their limit, a civil war to shuffle the public power is forced to happen. Additional to that, some historical boarder problems or island ownership issues are not solvable in short time as two to three years so that there do exist some hidden international wars.

在部分人民被壓迫到無法忍受的程度，內戰奪權就勢所難免。另外，歷史殘存的邊界問題或島嶼主權之爭也不是三兩年可以解決的所以潛伏的國際戰爭還在。

Nevertheless, consider all history of countries started by rebels, the ongoing event of Islamic State is the largest international "war of trouble time" territorially.

然而，縱觀游擊隊建國的例子，這個至今還沒有結束的伊斯蘭國事件，算是有史以來範圍最大的一個跨國"亂世戰爭"。

In a Chinese mind, "The world will divide after long unity, will unite after long separation.". They believe that a war will burst out in trouble time.

中國人認為"天下大勢合久必分，分久必合"。他們相信亂世必有戰爭。

In China, some bigger ones in the recorded wars of trouble
time are listed as the following: the Warring States era
from 476 to 221 BC, two Yellow Turban rebellions in Han
dynasty AD 184 and 188, the An-Shi rebellion in Tang
dynasty from AD 755 to 763, the LiangShanPo rebellion in
1119 and FangLa rebellion in 1120 and the Red Turban
rebellion in year 1351 of Song dynasty, the beginning of
Ming dynasty from 1367 to 1381, the ZhangXianZhong event
from 1630 to 1659, the TaiPing rebellion from 1850 to 1872,
the revolution of XinHai in 1911, the first civil war from
1927 to 1937, the World War II from 1937 to 1945, the
second civil war from 1945 to 1950, the Two-Two-Eight
event in 1947, the Three Anti-Campaign from 1951, the
bankruptcy of land owners in 1953, the Five-Anti-Campaign
from 1953 to 1956, Anti-Right-Campaign in 1957, the
Cultural Revolution from 1966 to 1976, the Formosa event
in 1979, Lin-Family event in 1980, Chen, Wen-Cheng event
in 1981, Jiang Nan event in 1984, Tian-An-Men event in
1989 and the ongoing Fa-Lun-Gong event from 1999 to now.
在中國，有歷史詳細記載的亂世戰爭，舉其大者有如下列：
西元前476年到221年的戰國時代，西元184年和188年東
漢靈帝的兩次黃巾之亂，755年到763年唐玄宗的安史之亂，
1119年北宋山東梁山泊的綠林造反，1120年明教方臘起義，
1351年白蓮教紅巾起事，1367年到1381年朱元璋起事，
1630年到1659年的張獻忠四川殘人事件，鴉片戰爭失敗後，
1850 年到 1872 年的天主教太平天國起事，1911 年辛亥革命，
1927年到1937年第一次國共內戰，1937年到1945年抗日戰
爭， 1945年到1950年第二次國共內戰，1947年二二八事件，
1951年東北三反運動，1953年地主破產，1953年到1956年
全國五反運動，1957年反右運動，1966年到1976年的文化
大革命，1979年美麗島事件，1980年林宅血案，1981年陳文
成命案，1984年江南命案，1989年天安門事件以及1999年
到現在的法輪功事件。

48

We may say that, before year 1911, the peaceful time was always ended by fatuous kings or tyrants; after 1911, it has been disappeared for longer than 100 years.

可以說，在 1911 年以前，中國的太平時期總是被昏君或暴君給結束掉；1911 後，中國的太平時期就暫時消逝了一百多年。

The extreme is the main role of wars in trouble time. Simply because they do things whole heartedly, do not care about their lives; never compromise and always insist the initial goal to the end.

極端份子是亂世戰爭的主角。只因為極端份子總是全心全意，不惜犧牲拼死拼活的做；不肯妥協，非做到底不可。

Some samples are "REAL" Judaists, Moslems, Protestants and Orthodox.. etc.. Their passions of pursuing eternal life is the highest level in the ball of LWJC.

例如"真正的"猶太教徒，伊斯蘭教徒，基督新教徒，東正教徒等等。他們對於永生的追求熱情是情爭義合球的最高階慾望。

However, each believer has different percentage of believing. Only those 100% believers are the extreme.
然而，每一個教徒的信仰程度都不一樣。信仰程度為 100%的教徒才是極端份子。

A strong believer of about 84% believing is one of the vigorous, about 67% is the sub-vigorous, about 50% is not a vigorous nor a non-vigorous, about 33% is a sub-non-vigorous, about 16% is a non-vigorous; while about 0%, is a person who does not care about the teaching, or claims as a believer under some other reason, and I think they should not be defined as a believer at all.

信仰程度為 84%左右的教徒是積極份子，67%
左右的是次積極份子，50%左右的是不積極也
不消極的人，33%左右的是次消極份子，16%左
右的是獨神教的消極份子；而 0%左右的，是
完全不在乎獨神教義的，或者完全為了其他目
的而宣稱自己是教徒的，應該是一個不算教徒
的教徒。

Relatively, the vigorous just do things
diligently. Normally, unless they have to
otherwise, they will not die for their goals.
They accept the fact and compromise with it;
just like Catholics who accept the Indulgence
and Sikhs who abandon discriminations; also
like the followers of Mozi and YangZhu.
相對的，積極份子只是勤快的做事。一般而言，除非
局勢所逼，他們不肯為目的而犧牲。他們接受實情，
能夠妥協；像承認大赦的天主教徒和不歧視的錫克教
徒；也像墨翟信徒和楊朱信徒。

3-3. Prejudice and
Balance (ZhongYong)
成見和平衡（中庸）

People with bias are the sub-vigorous. They have the third highest desire in the ball of LWJC, like Hindus, followers of Mencius and Xunzi,.. etc.. When the bias is deep enough and change to prejudice, the person is then close to the vigorous.

有偏見的人是次積極份子。他們有情爭義合球的第三高階慾望，像印度教徒，孟軻信徒和荀況信徒等等。偏見深了，如果變為成見，那個人就接近積極份子。

Confucius suggested that people should practice ZhongShu. ZhongShu means besides thinking about oneself people should consider the situation of others. This kind of people neither vigorous nor passive, their desire is the fourth highest level in the ball of LWJC.

孔子主張忠恕。忠恕是除了考慮自己的意願也能夠替對方設想的意思。這種人既不積極也不消極，他們的慾望是情爭義合球的第四高階慾望。

If a person has enough ability to find the balance point and solve a conflict; then, we are talking about the "high standard ZhongYong" taught by ZiSi. What Baha'i Belief wants is like that, they want to solve the conflicts among religions.
如果個人能力不錯，可以致中和，解決紛爭；那麼，我們現在所提到的就是子思所倡導的"高標準中庸之道"。巴哈伊信仰的主旨就是那樣，化解宗教糾紛。

However, there are two more ZhongYongZhiDao (the way of ZhongYong). One is an easy way of solving problems, the chairman/chairwoman of a meeting just let attendants provide their solutions then vote for decision; he/she can sit the chair firmly without making any error. The other way is quite the same as the "yielding" rule of Laozi, do not be the first in the world; but no sense of passiveness in it. That kind of ZhongYongZhiDao is the way of "MingZheBaoShen"; people should think hard (so that it is not passive), to figure out a non-vigorous solution to protect themselves.

但是，中庸之道還有另外兩種。一種是輕鬆的解決問題之道，會議主席只要讓出席的人提意見，然後，舉手表決；就可以穩坐首席，絕對不會出錯。另一種則接近老子的 "讓" 寶，不為天下先；可是完全沒有消極的意思。那個另一種中庸之道是 "明哲保身" 之道；需要動腦筋（所以不消極），去想一個 "不積極" 的自保方法。

3-4. Nature and Zen
自然和禪

The idea of Laozi was a kind of sub-passive. Although he mentioned about three precious rules, merciful, frugal and yielding; even a little further about returning good for evil and ZhongYongZhiDao; he always just used them for reference only. His main idea was "ruling with inaction", let all activities occur naturally.

老子的想法有點兒次消極。他雖然也提到三寶，慈儉讓，甚至大略提到以德報怨和中庸之道；但是他都只是說說而已。他的主要思想是"無為而治"，一切順其自然。

His sub-passive teaching simply suggested that officers should not pursue fame and benefits, so that people would not see anything desirable; hence people would cause fewer conflicts, then officers would have less trouble of handling law suits. His idea is the fifth highest, the third lowest, desire. 他那個次消極的教導只是指導官員不爭名利，讓人民不見可慾；人民自然少糾紛，官員也就減少訴訟的煩惱。他的主張是情爭義合球的第五高，第三低，的慾望。

The sixth master, HuiNeng, established the
Southern Zen, suggested everyone had a chance
to find oneself and own the absolute private
power to live in a complete true love. The
Zenists believe that people should see through
the activities in the world to discover and
protect ones true self. That is a passive view
of life. The teaching of HuiNeng is the sixth
highest, the second lowest, level in the ball
of LWJC.

六祖慧能創立南禪，主張人人都有機會頓悟，從而擁
有絕對的私權，生活在完整的真情裡頭。禪宗信徒相
信應該經由看透世情去發現並守護天生的自性。那是
一種消極的人生。慧能的教導，是情爭義合球的第六
高，第二低，的慾望。

3-5. The Emptiness of Buddha
佛陀的空

The idea of emptiness suggested by
Buddha was another end of the extreme.
Since all but emptiness, we can say
people really believe in him have no
desire at all.

佛陀的空是另一個極端。既然一切皆空，那麼真正相信佛陀的人沒有任何慾望。

Well, I believe that a person really has no desire may not exist. Suicide is a kind of desire. A person of hopeless still wants to live while an autistic person could have an unknown desire, strong or weak; I believe that if some of them have no desire at all then the number will be very limited.

我卻認為，真正沒有慾望的人也許並不存在。自殺可以算是一種願望。心灰意冷的失心人還希望活著而心封不傳的自閉人，他們的慾望可以或強或弱，外人不得而知；如果有些自閉人完全沒有慾望，我相信，人數也非常少。

I also believe that Buddha had stronger desire than that of Jesus. Jesus was crucified after three and half years of preaching; but, Buddha had preached for about forty-five years.

我還認為佛陀他自己，慾望比耶穌還強。耶穌宣揚自己的理想，才三年半就被釘死在十字架上；可是，佛陀講道，一講就是四十五年。

The enthusiasm to preach in the mind of Buddha was very strong. I think, the south pole and the north pole on my ball of LWJC could be one, "same point". Up to today, the only known person stand on that "same point" is Buddha. At the south pole, there is his theory and at the north pole there is the forty-year-long event of his preaching.

佛陀傳法渡人的意願非常強烈。我認為，我那個情爭義合球的南北兩極也許是"同一個點"；到目前為止，只有佛陀一個人在那"同一個點"上。在底下的是他的理論而在上面的是他歷時四十年的傳法事件。

The event closest to the preaching event of Buddha is the tragedy of preaching event done by Jesus. The "three and half years of tragedy", which happened on Jesus, deeply moves our souls.

最靠近佛陀傳法事件的是耶穌的傳法悲劇。耶穌那個"三年半的悲劇"深撼人心。

3-6. Insisting on extremity
堅持極端

The three extreme religions all ask
believers to have faith in God as
described in their respective Scriptures,
to do their best in understanding
Scriptures and to follow the rules as
required in Scriptures. By doing so,
they will enter the heaven after death.
極端的三個主要宗教都要求信徒相信各自經典
所描述的上帝，盡量去明白經典而且確實遵循
經典上所規定的儀軌。這樣做，死後才能進天
堂。

However, in Deuteronomy 13:5 of
their Bible and in Quran 2:193 both
mention about that, the prophet (or
dreamer) must be put to death for
inciting rebellion against the God.
然而，他們的聖經申命記 13：5 和可蘭
經 2：193 都提到，如果看到宣揚異教的
先知（或夢者）必須將他處死。

Although they would kill prophets only
and let followers go; I think the way of
killing "Pagans" is still too extreme.
雖然他們只殺先知，放過異教徒；我認為殺死
某些"異教人"的做法仍然太極端了。

Within each of the three
religion groups there are more
or less of internal conflicts;
so that it is even harder for
the three to work together.
這三個宗教多少都有內亂問題；所以
彼此更加無法相容。

First of all, both of the teachings of
Judaism and Islamism do not believe
Jesus is the son of God. They do not
really believe the Spirit neither.
第一，猶太教和伊斯蘭教的教義都不相信耶穌
是神的兒子。他們也不真相信有聖靈這個東西。

Secondly, the believers of Judaism insist they are the chosen people of God, the New Testament is not the words of God. But Christians believe Jesus is the son of God. They think in the New Testament God already changed the chosen people from Jews to people who believe in Jesus. Whether a person is one of the chosen people or not will be dicided on the judgement day when Jesus comes again.

第二，猶太教徒堅持他們是上帝的選民，認為新約聖經不是上帝的話。可是相信耶穌是神子的基督徒卻認為，在新約裡頭上帝已經把選民改為相信耶穌是神子的人們；而誰是上帝的選民將在耶穌再次降臨的審判日揭曉。

Among Christians, Lutherans believe in justification by faith, whoever believe in Jesus will have eternal celestial glory. Calvinists believe that people know God deeply via Spirit; however, knowing God does not guarantee an eternal life in heaven.

其中，路德宗認為因信稱義，相信耶穌者可以得永生。加爾文宗則明確的說，因聖靈的感應，信耶穌者得以深信上帝；可是，上不上天堂仍然是上帝的特權。

The third, Moslems believe Mohammed was
the last prophet, the Quran he acquired
is a correction that God did to the New
Testament. According to Quran, God has
no son. Moslems believe that Jesus is
simply a prophet, same as Mohammed.
第三，伊斯蘭教徒卻認為，穆罕默德是最後的
先知，他傳達的可蘭經是上帝對新約聖經所做
的更正。根據可蘭經，上帝沒有兒子。伊斯蘭
教徒相信耶穌和穆罕默德一樣，只是一個先知。

Moslems believe in both of God and the prophet,
pray five times a day, give money to the poor
as they can, observe the holy month of Ramadan
and try pilgrimage to Mecca at least once in a
lifetime if one is able. The Five Pillars is
their way to the heaven.
伊斯蘭信徒既相信主也相信使者，每日做五次禮拜，
做自力可及的施捨，遵守齋戒月和努力嘗試一生至少
一次的麥加朝覲。這五功是他們上天堂的道路。

The Five Pillars is able to secure an eternal life in
the heaven without being a follower of Judaism nor
believing Jesus is the son of God. Because the Five
Pillars is achievable to most people, Moslems is the
second largest religious groups now.

五功就可以保證永生，既不需要歸依猶太教也不必相信耶穌是神的兒子。因為五功是多數人辦得到的要求，所以伊斯蘭教逐漸發展成今天的第二大宗教。

3-7. Three Religions Stand Firmly
三教鼎立

Because of being not compatible to each other, within same belief, different denominations have conflicts on the goal of absorbing more believers, and the competition is stronger between different believes; besides that, it is unpreventable that they will fight for the Holy City.

因為不相容，所以同一個信仰的不同派別之間在爭取更多信徒的目標上必定相互衝突，更別說不同信仰的派別；而且，彼此爭奪同一聖城的事也在所難免。

Analyzing from the religious situation today, The protestants and Orthodox are stronger financially while Moslems are stronger doctrine wise. The remained believers of Judaism have been the strongest financially but weakest doctrine wise due to their narrow teachings.

從今日宗教世界的實際情況來分析，基督新教和東正教教徒佔了財務上的優勢而伊斯蘭教徒佔了教義上的優勢。另一方面，猶太教徒則一向佔有最高的財務優勢，卻又一向屈居最劣勢的狹隘教義。

If we base on this analysis to prospect the next decade, the "money first" period from 2015 to 2025, the economic pressure will decide the direction of the change.

從這個分析去做十年預期，在"金錢掛帥"的2015年到2025年，經濟壓力將決定世局走向。

When part of citizens are oppressed to their limit, a civil war for the public power will follow.
在部分人民被壓迫到無法忍受的程度，內戰奪權就勢所難免。

There are more or less of people insist the extremity and the leader of the IS event is just one of rebellion leaders in many "war of trouble time". He was born 1971 in Iraq, after finished his PhD thesis on theology he married in 2000 then had a son about 12 years ago. He established JJASJ in 2003 and was appointed the chief of sharia committee; he was incarcerated in 2004. When the JJASJ merged to MSC in 2006, he was a member of sharia committee; then MSC was changed to ISI in the same year and he was the head of sharia committee again. On 4/8/2013 he was named the caliph of ISIL. On 6/29/2014 ISIL expanded to IS and he was still the caliph.

每一個地方都有或多或少堅持極端的人而伊斯蘭國事件的主角就是許多 "亂世戰爭" 的叛逆首領之一。他生於 1971 年的伊拉克，獲神學博士後在 2000 年結婚，得一子今年 12 歲。他在 2003 年建立了 JJASJ，擔任審判委員會會長；曾在 2004 年被關。然後在 2006 年 JJASJ 加入 MSC，他降為委員；MSC 在同年改名 ISI 後，他又從委員升為審判委員會會長。2013 年 4 月 8 日，他當上 ISIL 的政教首領。2014 年 6 月 29 日 ISIL 擴充成為 IS，他仍然是 IS 的政教首領。

Just like the government of Taliban, IS government adopted the whole Sharia. Saudi Arabia adopt the main idea of Sharia while a judge has right to interpret Sharia. In Iran their culture just orders that the laws cannot contradict Sharia.

和塔利班政府一樣，伊斯蘭國採用全部的伊斯蘭教法，Sharia（雪利亞）。沙烏地阿拉伯採用它的主要概念，法官有權解釋 Sharia。而伊朗只是規定法律不得違背伊斯蘭教法。

3-8. Belief and King
信仰和國王

Due to limitation of their knowledge, people need an ultimate belief. Due to the gregarious instinct, people need a political king. So, at each corner of the world, people started their developments all from a few Gods and a few kings. 由於知識有限，人類需要終極信仰。由於群居天性，人類需要政治國王。於是，在全球各地，人類社會一律從少神少王開始發展。

Around 500 BC, some different cultures were established. Some of special cultures were a few Gods and one king in Persia, the love-God culture; many Gods and many kings in Classical Athens, the democratic culture; a few Gods and one king in India, the become-God culture; many Gods and one theocrat in Maya and Yoruba, the theocratic culture and all ancestors with one king in China, the monarchical culture.

到了西元前 500 年左右，在世界各地產生了幾個不同的文化系統。比較特別的有波斯帝國的少神一王，愛神文化；雅典的多神多王，民主文化；印度的少神一王，成神文化；馬雅人和約魯巴人的多神一王，神權文化和中國的眾祖一王，君主文化。

When it was around 300 BC, Macedon terminated the Classical Athens and started the many Gods and one king, the monarchical culture, while the king of India promoted zero God one king, the Buddhism culture.
到了西元前 300 年左右，雅典被馬其頓消滅改為多神一王的君主文化，而印度則推廣無神一王的佛陀文化。

Let us jump into year 800, the three Gods (the Father, the Son and the Spirit) and a few kings in Rome at Europe replaced Macedon, created the respect-God culture; India changed back to a few Gods and one king, monarchical culture while frequently affected by the mid-east culture; the new mid-east one God and one king culture in Abbasid Caliphate is the caliph culture of united religion and politics.
我們跳到西元 800 年，馬其頓文化被歐洲的羅馬帝國三神（聖父，聖子和聖靈）少王的敬神文化取代；印度又回到少神一王的君主文化而經常受到中亞文化的影響；新的中亞文化則是阿拔斯王朝，神王合一的卡里發文化。

The Tang dynasty of China remained as all ancestors and one king, the monarchical culture with one more branch of knowledge, Zenism, additional to the original two, Confucianism and Taoism. Both of Maya and Yoruba cultures were quite unchanged.

中國唐朝則在士大夫之間的百家學問，由原來的兩大家，道家和儒家，變成三大家，多了釋家；仍然是眾祖一王君主文化。馬雅文化和約魯巴文化也大致沒有改變。

About religion, in 1054 a two Gods (the Father and the Spirit) and one king, the Orthodoxy respect-God culture, started in north Europe; in 1527 a One Guiding God (the Son, Lutheranism) and one king, the Protestantism trust-God culture started in Europe; in 1541, one more new Protestantism, Calvinism started; in 1559 another Protestantism, Puritan, started. In 1620 some separatists of Puritan moved to north America. In 1698 three Gods Protestantism, Anglicanism, started in England. There were a few more Protestantism churches started after 1559.

在宗教上，1054 年北歐增加了兩神（聖父和聖靈）
一王的東正宗敬神文化。1527 年歐洲增加了一導神
（聖子，信義宗）一王的基督新教信神文化；1541
年，多了歸正宗信神文化；1559 年多了清教徒信神
文化。1620 年清教徒分離派移居到北美洲。1698 年
基督新教又多了聖公宗敬神文化。其他在 1559 年以
後產生的基督新教信神文化也不少。

About politics, in 1215 England started
a new three Gods and a few kings, the
democratic culture; in 1689 it changed
to three Gods and many kings, the
democratic culture; after 1698 Anglicans
changed it to three God and all kings
gradually, the constitutional
monarchical culture. In 1776 Americans
established one Guiding God and all
kings, the elected-president democratic
culture. After year 1945, American
culture have been spread all over the
world via its silver bullets. With help
of two new custodians later on, the
prosperous American culture has been
growing, up to today, 3/31/2015.

在政治上，1215 年英國建立新的三神少王，
民主文化；1689 年改為三神多王，民主文化；
1698 年以後逐漸改為由聖公宗帶頭的一神眾
王，君主立憲民主文化。1776 年美國建立新
的一神眾王，總統直選民主文化。1945 年以
後，美國文化逐漸在全球透過銀彈四處散播。
因為後來又添了兩大護法天將所以直到今天，
2015-3-31，漲勢未消。

3-9. Technology and Computer as Custodians
科技和電腦護法天將

In year 1942 the American Manhattan Project
brought the world a new custodian for the
spirit of competition, the technology
custodian. Then in 1995, the world wide web
brought the world another new custodian for
the spirit of competition, the computer
custodian. Then America finally established a
democratic culture of one Guiding God, two
custodians and all kings with Protestantism,
technology and computer.

1942 年美國的曼哈頓計劃為全世界引進了一個競爭精神的護法天將，科技護法；1995 年全球網路又為全世界引進了一個新的競爭精神的護法天將，電腦護法。於是美國終於完成一個包含新教，科技和電腦的一導神二將眾王的民主文化。

While Incas in south America expanded from around year 1200, established a kingdom in 1438 and disappeared in 1533; Aztecs expanded from around year 1325, established a kingdom in 1428 and disappeared in 1521; the Maya culture disappeared in 1441 after its long existence, as well.
而南美的印加人從 1200 年擴展，在 1438 年建國到 1533 年消逝；阿茲特克人從 1325 年擴展，在 1428 年建國到 1521 年消逝；歷史比較長久的馬雅文化也在 1441 年消逝。

China suddenly changed to an all ancestors and all kings, a democratic culture, in 1911 then changed to an all ancestors and one party, a mono-party culture in year 1945.
在 1911 年中國突然變成眾祖眾王的民主文化而在 1945 年改成眾祖一黨的獨黨文化。

About culture, after year 1945, many countries
have changed to various "all kings"
democratic cultures, including the area Taiwan
which is not recognized as a country.
在文化上，1945 年以後，許多國家都逐漸改為"眾
王"的多種類型的民主文化，包括非國家，台灣在內。

About other influences from the American
culture, we may see it via two custodians.
至於美國文化的其他影響，可以用兩個天將來說明。

The custodian started earlier is the
technology which has automated the
production lines for many countries.
People do not constantly "exhaust
muscular power" to work anymore, so
that they are away from "muscular body
and powerful strength" farther and
farther now.
首先出現的科技天將把許多國家的生產線給自
動化了。人類不再需要經常"出大力"去工作，
所以人類離"身強力健"越來越遠。

The custodian started later is the computer related devices adopted by USA and other developed countries to control workers. Many organizations are vigorously analyzing computer data to increase output of their teams. Bosses do not "apply true heart" to encourage workers anymore, so that they are away from "heartfelt love and firm justice" farther and farther now.

後來出現的電腦天將則在美國和其他已開發國家，被用來控制員工。許多機構正積極使用電腦記錄來增加團隊的工作效率。老闆們，不再需要"用真心"去激勵員工，所以老闆們離"有情重義"越來越遠。

In year 2015, the so-called LEAN and WFO are using the super tool, WEBSITES, and the fake banner, RESPECT, to enter more and more big companies and governments gradually.

到了 2015 年，所謂企業瘦身（LEAN）和極化勞動力（WFO）正假借尊重（RESPECT）這個虛假名義，利用電腦網站（WEBSITES）這個超級工具，逐漸進駐了越來越多的大公司和政府機構。

4. Brain and Heart
理智與情感

Besides the different depths of
clearness on feelings, people
also have higher or lower of
different intelligences.
Everyone is different.
除了情感上的慧根深淺，人類還有理
智上的高低之分。每個人都不一樣。

Besides the difference of love between
genders which I mentioned in 2-2, above
two aspects of wisdom greatly make the
"Equalitarianism" against to nature.
除了 2-2 提到的男女情衷有別，上述智慧的兩
項差異更加讓 "平等主義" 大大的違背自然。

Besides cannot but age, cannot but die, people also
cannot but confuse. Being confused, the best people
can say is some superficial theory about here and now.
除了不能不老，不能不死，人類還不能不惑。不能不惑，就
是只能說說一時一地的粗淺道理。

That means, including some of my opinions, the freedom of speech only increases some dubious biases in most cases.
所以，包括某些我的意見，言論自由往往只是給歷史增加了一些不三不四的偏見而已。

In a gregarious environment, a person has to be influenced by others. So-called "Liberalism" is basically not practical.
在群居的環境，一個人不能不受他人影響。所謂"自由主義"根本就不實際。

Quite the same Bible, it created two largest religious groups which are fighting each other to death. That fact let the "Philanthropism" claimed by the religions of God-loves-people becomes seriously inconsistent in words and deeds.

類似的聖經，卻產生了目前正戰得你
死我活的全球兩個最大宗教。這個事
實讓"博愛主義"在愛人類的宗教裡
頭徹頭徹尾，言行不一。

4-1. So-called Wisdom
所謂智慧

When people make a choice for a problem,
"intelligence" let them know the
related facts while "clearness on
feelings" let people know the main
point of their wishes.
在人們對一個問題做出選擇的時候，"智"讓
人們了解到相關的事實真相而"慧"讓人們看
清楚自己的心意重點。

However, people may have either nice or evil intent
for an event; hence no matter how high could the
wisdom of people go, there is no guarantee that the
ideal world people wished will be secured in some way.
但是，人在事前的存心有好有壞；所以人們的智慧再高，也
無法保證人們所期待的理想世界能夠長存。

So-called wisdom:
所謂智慧：

The wisest people are named saints
(the wise) or devil (the evil);
people with the next level of
wisdom are named the smart
(including virtuous officers and
credible merchants) or the
treacherous (including corruptive
officer and dishonest traders).
最有智慧的人叫做聖人或梟雄；其次叫
做賢人（包括廉臣和信商）或奸人（包括貪
官和謊商）。

The further down is named the vulgar,
there are of cause some nice guys and
some bad guys among the vulgar; then
people at one more level down are named
nincompoops or scoundrels.
再其次叫做凡人，凡人自然也有好的凡人和壞
的凡人；更其次的叫做愚人或惡棍。

People at the lowest level of wisdom are
called the hopeless. There are two kinds of
hopeless people, one who voluntarily give up
all hopes and the other kind who seal their
mind passively by different reasons. Nobody
knows the hope of a hopeless person.
最低智慧的人叫做灰人。灰人分為主動心死的灰人和因不同
理由而被動心封的灰人。沒有人知道灰人的希望。

Among the hopeless, some are quiet and
easy going, the good ones; while some
others are active and trouble making,
the bad ones.
在灰人裡頭，有安靜而容易照顧的好灰人；也
有活躍而常惹麻煩的壞灰人。

5. Design and Result
計劃與結果

There is a saying in China states "Do your best, wait for fate." You plan and do it, but the result depends on your luck. 中國人說 "盡人事，聽天命"。計劃總是要做，結果就看個人造化。

So-called "Be prepared." is just because "A danger foreseen is half avoided.". Since it is impossible for people to prepare for all 100% details so that if there will be danger or not still depends on personal luck. That is what stated in a Chinese proverb "People do their best, the heaven makes its decision."

所謂 "有備無患" 只是因為 "人無遠慮，必有近憂" 而已。人們不可能準備得百分之百周全；所以究竟有沒有患，還得看個人運氣。也就是中國諺語說的 "盡事在人，成事在天"。

Nevertheless, in an eternal culture, the fate is clearly written into words on their Scriptures or Bibles. So, whatever they should do is clearly listed in all kinds of Scriptures.

然而，在永恆的文化裡頭，天命已經白紙黑字寫在經上。所以，他們該做的事都已經詳細的列在各種經典裡頭。

No matter how the world changes, the change is just a minor issue to true believers of God. To them, the result is decided and it will not change any more.

無論世界如何變化，對神的真誠教徒來說，都只是小事一樁。對他們來說，結果已經確定再也不會變更。

6. Thirteen levels of Virtue
十三品人

In the book "Lorentz Transformation for High School Students" I mentioned about my idea of thirteen levels of virtue.

在 "Lorentz Transformation for High School Students" 那一本書裡頭，我提出十三品人的看法。

I divided people into thirteen levels from high to low in spirit, or in the quality of souls.

我把人類的精神，或靈魂的品質，分為上下十三等級。

The highest level belongs to people with top affection and top logic. Most of them are low key, not famed people.

最上品的是至情至理的人。他們絕大多數是不欲人知，默默無名的低調人。

Then, following the order are people with top affection and much logic, much affection and top logic, much affection and much logic, much logic and enough affection and then much affection and enough logic.
然後，依序是至情足理，足情至理，足情足理，足理有情以及足情有理。

The next level, the seventh level, the enough affection and enough logic level belongs to most lovely and common people.
接下來的第七品，有情有理，就是一般平凡可愛的人們。

After that we have people with enough affection and weak logic, enough logic and weak affection, weak affection and weak logic, weak affection and no logic, weak logic and no affection and then the worst level of no affection and no logic.
然後是有情弱理，有理薄情，薄情弱理，薄情無理，弱理無情和最下品的無情無理。

7. Health and Hopes
健康與希望

My definition of health is very simple, if I can do what I most want to do, then my body is "healthiest".

我對身體健康的定義很簡單，能夠做自己最想做的事，身體就"最健康"。

The next level is, if I can do what I secondly or thirdly want to do, then my body is "luckily healthy".

其次，能夠做自己第二或第三想做的事，就有"幸運的健康"。

The further down is, if I can do at least one thing I like to do, like taking a warm shower, eating a delicious dinner, listening to a nice performance or seeing a wonderful picture, or like writing a letter to a friend, visiting a forgotten relative, having a sunbath in a winter,.. etc.; then my body is "appreciatively healthy".

再其次，至少能夠做一件自己喜歡做的事，好比洗個熱水澡，吃一頓美味的晚餐，聽一段好演奏或者看一幅好畫，又或者寫一封給朋友的信，拜訪久違的一個親友，曬個冬天的太陽等等；那就有"感恩的健康"。

Yes, the first kind of hopeless people with a dead will and the second kind of hopeless people who are unable to communicate with others are the unhealthy "hopeless people". The second kind of hopeless people may have some hope but they need help to keep alive while the helpers are unable to know their hopes.

是的，心灰意冷的第一類灰人和無法與他人溝通的第二類灰人，是不健康的"灰者"。第二類灰者可能有某些希望但是他們需要幫忙維持生活而照顧者無法知道他們的希望。

I believe that hope is the source of health.
我認為希望是健康之母。

8. Chances
機會

I believe that chances exist at every single minute; because I am able to make a different choice for my life at any time.
我認為機會存在於每一個時刻；因為我隨時可以對我的人生做出不同的抉擇。

However, whether I should move or wait, it depends on my wisdom, true heart and bravery at that time.
然而，是動是靜，但憑當時的智慧，仁心和勇氣。

8-1. Event
事件

An event includes a series of choices and some lucks.
一個事件包括一串抉擇和一些運氣。

How many "big" events can happen to the whole life of one person?
一個人的一生能夠有多少 "大" 事件?

The "biggest" event is when a great person does something benefits people. For example, a leader handled an unavoidable disaster with minimum loss or a doctor controlled a pestilence or cured a disease. Or like the inventor of modern toilet and the inventor of printing, telephone, refrigerator and inventors of computer.

一個偉人，做了一些對人類有益的事，那是
"最大"的事。好比，領袖以最小的死傷解決
無法避免的災難或者是醫生對傳染病的控制或
對疾病的治療。又好比現代馬桶的發明人以及
印刷，電話，電冰箱的發明人乃至於電腦的發
明人。

Secondly, an artist completes some
fine arts is also a "big" event.
Like the works of Laozi, Goethe,
Beethoven and Da Vinci as well as
good sounds, dances and movies.
其次，一個藝術家完成一些美妙作品，
那也是"大"事。好比老子，歌德，貝
多芬和達文奇的作品和好歌舞，好電影。

Then, is to bear and raise a great
person or a wonderful artist considered
a "big" event? I think, it is
necessary to mention about parents.

那麼，生下並養大一個偉人或好藝術家算不算
一件 "大" 事？我想，父母的簡介是必要的。

As to assist a great person or artist in
completing "a big event", I think, it is at
least an important plot; should be included in
the record of that big event.
至於協助一個偉人或藝術家完成 "一件大事"，我想，
至少是一個重要的情節；應當包括在那件大事的記錄
裡頭。

A historical event has a beginning, the story and an
ending in the recorded time; but, an scientific event
has only one event time. In case we should make it
clear I use "story" for a "historical event" or a
series of "scientific event".
歷史事件，在時刻上有頭有身有尾；但是，科學事件只有一
個事件時刻。有必要區分時我用一個 "故事" 來代表一個
"歷史事件" 或一串 "科學事件"。

8-2. Yoichi Hatta
八田與一

Yoichi Hatta built the Wushantou Damand and his wife, Panevico tree, committed suicide for love were two "big" events.

八田與一興建烏山頭水庫事件和他的夫人，外代樹，自殺殉夫事件就是兩個"大"事。

The Ball of LWJC

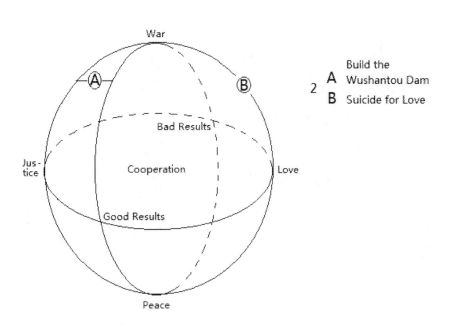

In my opinion, the first event, event A, was an event of secondly strong, for justice, with a good result. It is an event of benefiting people done by a great man.

Another event, event B, was an event of secondly strong, for love, with an ending of no goodness and no badness. That is an event of love story done by an artist.

情爭義合球

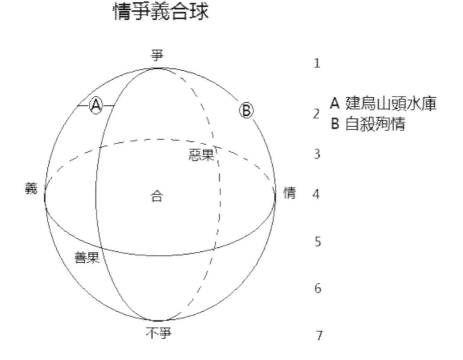

我認為，第一個事件，事件 A，是第二強烈，為了公義，有善果的大事。那是一個偉人的造福事跡。

另一個事件，事件 B，是第二強烈，為了私情，無善無惡的大事。那是一個藝術家的愛情事跡。

8-3. Your Major Events
你的重要事跡

You may review five biggest events in your life, analyze the strength level of related desire, the percentage of your purpose for love and justice and then the result of them as how much of good and bad; just write each of them briefly.
你不妨回顧你最大的五個事件，分析慾望的等級，情義的成分以及結果的善惡；摘要描述每一個事件。

It may bring some fun, do you like to try it?
那也許是有趣的事，要不要試試看？

The Ball of LWJC

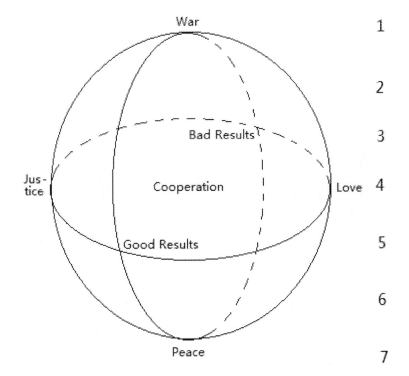

So far, your biggest event is:

_____

_____

_____

_____

_____

_____

_____

_____

情爭義合球

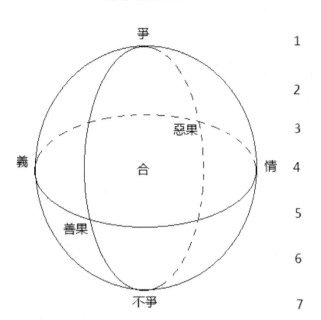

爭　　　　　　1

　　　　　　　2

惡果　　　　　3

義　　合　情　4

　　　　　　　5

善果　　　　　6

不爭　　　　　7

到目前為止，你的最大事跡是：

_____

_____

_____

_____

_____

_____

_____

_____

_____

The Ball of LWJC

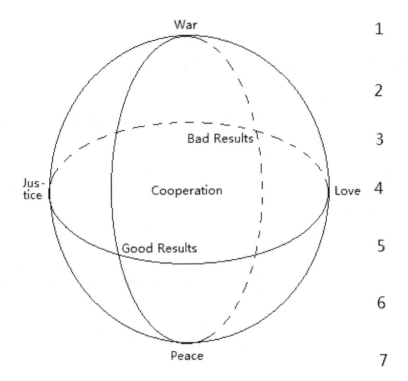

The second of your big events is:

_____

_____

_____

_____

_____

_____

_____

_____

情爭義合球

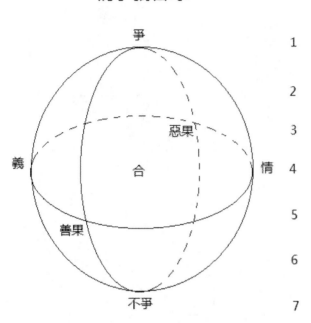

争

1

2

惡果

3

義 合 情 4

5

善果

6

不爭 7

104

你的第二大事跡是：

_____

_____

_____

_____

_____

_____

_____

_____

The Ball of LWJC

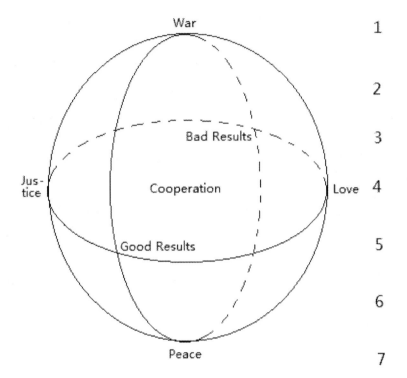

War

Bad Results

Jus-
tice   Cooperation   Love

Good Results

Peace

1

2

3

4

5

6

7

The third of your big events is:

_____

_____

_____

_____

_____

_____

_____

_____

情爭義合球

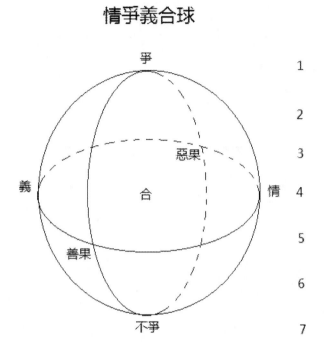

爭　　　　　　1

　　　　　　　2

惡果　　　　　3

義　　合　　情　4

　　　　　　　5

善果

　　　　　　　6

不爭　　　　　7

你的第三大事跡是：

_____

_____

_____

_____

_____

_____

_____

_____

The Ball of LWJC

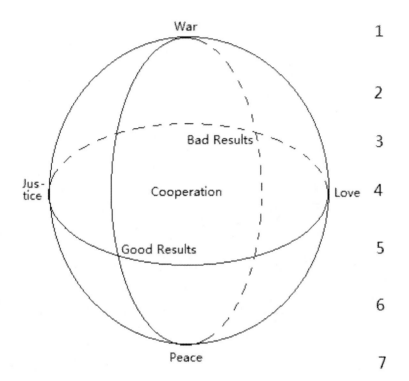

The fourth of your big events is:

_____

_____

_____

_____

_____

_____

_____

_____

情爭義合球

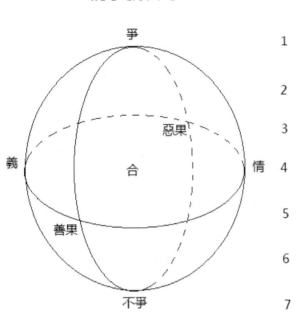

你的第四大事跡是：

_____

_____

_____

_____

_____

_____

_____

_____

_____

The Ball of LWJC

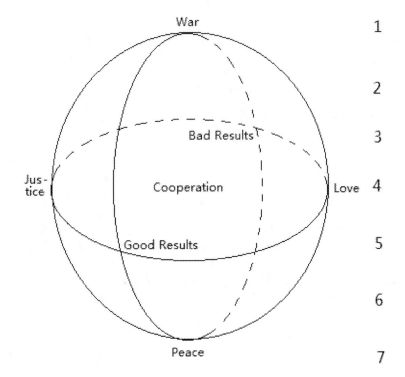

The fifth of your big events is:

_____

_____

_____

_____

_____

_____

_____

情爭義合球

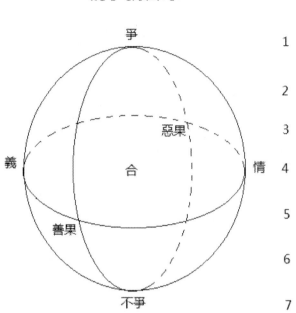

你的第五大事迹是：

_____

_____

_____

_____

_____

_____

_____

_____

_____

8-4. Global Events
全球事件

What are the five biggest global events in the recorded history? Or, I should ask, what are the five greatest person and five most wonderful artists in the recorded history? Why?

在歷史裡頭全球最大的五個事件是哪些？或者，我該問的是，有史以來最偉大的五個人是誰而最出色的五個藝術家又是誰？為什麼？

For great people I will select from the following list: the person tried successfully in keeping fire alive, tried successfully in starting a fire, tried successfully in organizing a language, farming livestock, farming crops, organizing a corresponding set of characters for the language; inventing paper, printing books, bringing in electricity, inventing a flush toilet, inventing camera (after about 2240 years since Mocius noticed the phenomena of camera obscura), inventing phonograph cylinder, inventing movie, inventing radio, inventing refrigerator, inventing TV, inventing computer and internet...etc.. How about you, one of kings in the democratic government?

我心目中的偉人包括成功讓火苗長存的人，成功生火的人，成功整理語言的人，開始蓄牧，耕種，整理文字；發明紙，印刷術，電，抽水馬桶，照相機（在墨翟發現暗箱現象大約 2240 年後），留聲機，電影，無線廣播，電冰箱，電視，電腦和網路，，等等。身為民主政府萬王之一的您，選誰呢？

Most inventions are results of personal efforts however inventors must stand on the shoulders of earlier inventors.
雖然多數的發明是個人努力的結果但是發明家必須依靠早期發明家所累積的知識和經驗。

For most wonderful artists in the recorded history, ah, there are too many. In my mind, the best kind of artists are people who solve a conflict without war and make no harm to both parties and any third party or at least, with minimum damages.
至於最出色的藝術家，啊，太多了。在我心目中，最好的那種藝術家是不戰而解決紛爭的人；不傷害爭執雙方，也不傷害任何第三者或者讓損傷減到最低。

As I can tell, quite a few of such most wonderful artists are hiding behind the scene; and in some cases, there are more than one artist get involved in an event of conflict, especially a war.
就我所知，上述那種藝術家有不少人是隱身幕後的；有時候，在一個抗爭事件，尤其在一場戰爭中，還有不少藝術家參與其間。

8-5. Baha'i Entrepreneurs Bridging Association (BEBA)
巴哈伊助立橋（巴橋）

If you are retired and want to do something good, you may join Baha'i Entrepreneurs Bridging Association (BEBA) which will start no later than 6/1/2016. The purpose of BEBA is to create healthy and stable jobs for people.

如果您已經退休卻想做點兒好事，不妨加入在 2016 年 6 月 1 日前必定成立的巴哈伊助立橋（巴橋）。巴橋的目的是創造健康而穩定的工作。

Why did I name it a Baha'i Bridge? My idea is to build a bridge for religious people and non-religious people to communicate with each other and then allow them to work together.

為什麼我把它叫做巴橋呢？我的想法是搭一座橋讓信神的人和不信神的人可以互相連絡從而一起工作。

I have collected $3.06 to fund BEBA as of 2/10/2015 which is 60% of $5.06, my first royalty check paid by Trafford, after tax. I had published 8 books since year 2005 and this is my last book with Trafford. I am going to donate 60% of my royalty from all 9 books, after tax, to BEBA. Hope my donation will increase considerably before 6/1/2016.

我在 2015 年 2 月 10 日收到出版社的第一次版權費 5.06 美元， 稅後的百分之六十大約是 3.06 美元。從 2005 年以來我一共在這家出版社出版了 8 本書而這一本是第 9 本。我決定把這 9 本書的版權費的稅後 60%捐給巴橋。希望我的捐款在 2016 年 6 月 1 日前能夠激增。

If I cannot find a leader for BEBA before 6/1/2016 I will be the lead for BEBA until someone takes over.

如果我在 2016 年 6 月 1 日前無法給巴橋找到領袖，我就自己當，一直到有人接棒。

What BEBA will do is quite the same as the Seattle-Taiwanese Entrepreneurs-Promoting Association (STEPA) described in my previous book "The Definition of Spacetime", except BEBA will be a global group while STEPA, if it will start, will be a local group.

巴橋要做的事和在"時空的定義"所介
紹的西雅圖助立社要做的事很像，不同
處只在巴橋是全球的團體而西雅圖助立
社是地方團體。

8-6. STEPA
西雅圖助立社

Here is a brief introduction of STEPA, Seattle-Taiwanese
Entrepreneurs-Promoting Association.

Seattle-Taiwanese Entrepreneurs-Promoting Association is a
group to be organized soon. In my mind, the members of STEPA
are Taiwanese who have stable economic support either retired or
a business owner in Seattle area. STEPA members do not pay any
fee and there is no office for STEPA. The chief board member will
decide how long is that position and the list of all members as well
as projects reports are all in a free website to be decided.

The purpose of STEPA is to work together for providing jobs.

That means, since being established, members of
STEPA like to help establishing people.

The way STEPA works is to create all kinds of special business
groups, like SEAA in 10-1, to find prospective established
business owners who want to start a special business based on the
wage system of clean & abled management and the principle of
reinvestment.

Wage system: clean & abled management

The hourly wage and the benefits of a frontline worker is the same as average from same kind of jobs in the local area.

The lead-worker is a frontline worker who is also responsible for on-job training and handling emergency conditions like absent without notice and time sensitive issues so that the treatment is 105% of the highest treatment of frontline workers under the lead.

All other managers are paid average of wage and benefits of all workers directly report to the manager.

Profit distribution: no more than 15%

In the first 5 years, no more than 5% of profit can be distributed to stock holders; it will be no more than 10% of profit from the 6th year to the 10th year, then, no more than 15% after that. The rest of profit should be used to improve the business or open new branches.

8-6-1. Seattle virtuous-Events and wonderful-Arts Association (SEAA)

Select an owner of Chinese newspaper in Seattle area like Asia Today, Seattle Chinese Post, Chinese Seattle News (Washington Chinese post, Seattle Chinese Journal) and Seattle Chinese Times etc. or a person with leadership be the chief board member of SEAA and I will be the contact person. The purpose of SEAA is to create a business named Great virtuous-Events and Great wonderful-Arts Weekly Inc. (GeGaWI) to publish a weekly magazine named GeGa Weekly to report the practical events as defined in the section 9-9 for two kinds of information only. There are three stages:

Stage 1: I will look for the starting members, including the chief board member, then the chief board member registers the foundation with 52% of the total investment and other founding members contribute the rest 48%.

Stage 2: Find an established Chinese newspaper or magazine like Taiwan News, Epoch News or Commonwealth Magazine etc. to create GeGaWI with two to three sponsors like stated in details on page 115 and the following pages.

Stage 3: Sold GeGaWI to Google or other international big company so that GeGa Weekly will belong to the new GeWeekly or XeWeekly to make itself a global magazine.

8-6-2. GeGa Weekly

A proposal of GeGa Weekly
好妙周刊草案
by SEAA （西雅圖好妙社）

Great virtuous-Events and Grate
wonderful-Arts Weekly Inc.
GeGaWI, 好妙周刊社

Purpose:

The main purpose of creating GeGaWI and its branch offices is to create decent editor's and translator's jobs for more and more people via publishing GeGa Weekly. 成立 GeGaWI 利用好妙周刊提供溫飽的編輯工作。

What is GeGa Weekly?

GeGa Weekly is a weekly newspaper about PRACTICAL news. All news provided by PeWeekly must be at least 7 days old. The report must be practically useful and must base on fact, promote kindness and justice, 守真, 揚善, 求義.

How GeGa Weekly work?

The workers at GeGa Weekly believe that they will make mistakes so that when subscribers correct mistakes in reports, those actions will receive some editing reward-points. The report summaries are free to everyone but the details are available for subscribers only.

A common guide line:

Chinese people believe that people should focus on current life and current world only. They try to make the current world an ideal world, named "DaTong-ShiJie", where their offspring may enjoy. They don't know how long can souls (or ghosts) live.

Hindu and Buddhist believe in transmigration of souls and wish their souls could escape from the current troublesome world to a peaceful land. Catholic, Christian and Moslem believe in one God and wish their souls will stay with God in the heaven after they die.

Although people believe in different religious teachings and wish for different future of their souls, they all agree on the common guide line that people should find the truth, do good things and appreciate beauties, especially internal beauties.
人類的共同行為方針：尋真，行善，賞美，尤其是內在美。

Plans:

Plan 1: GeGa Weekly will provide free commercial for one to three selected business partners like IKEA and I-Mei Foods Co., LTD (IMEI) …(to be decided). GeGa Weekly will also provide a small area for paid commercials and GeGa Weekly will verify the commercials before put them on the website. All branch offices of GeGa Weekly will verify all commercials too.

Plan 2: At the first five years, GeGa Weekly and its branch offices will distribute local practical news related to science, politics/laws, and arts, especially NEW events related to HARMONIC HUMAN SOCIETIES, and try to support themselves by all kinds of verified commercials and the membership income from subscribers.

Plan 3: Five years later, they will start to design some local projects to enhance local harmonic environments with other related groups. GeGa Weekly will also try to sell itself to Google or other influential international company with the condition that Epoch Times will be one of the three business partners which will occupy the commercial position of education as shown in the following figure.

Commercial Income:

Besides subscribers' payment GeGa Weekly will use the bottom space which is 20% (or 25%, 33% to be enlarged) of the whole screen to sell commercials. At the upper left corner, 1/10 of the bottom space is reserved for IKEA, at the upper right corner, 1/10 of the bottom space is reserved for IMEI. Besides IKEA, two 1/10 of the bottom spaces are open to clothing related businesses. Under IKEA, there is one 1/10 space open to housing related businesses. In the center area, the upper 1/10 space is open to education related business and the 1/10 space under it is open to entertainment related business. Tow 1/10 spaces connected to IMEI are open to food related businesses and the last 1/10 space is open to transportation related business.

However, all the 10 available spaces are all open in the homepages of branch offices in related areas. The reserved areas for IKEA and IMEI will not show up on the local homepages unless they pay for it.

The representatives of IKEA and IMEI may work at GeGa Weekly when the branch offices of GeGa Weekly is more than 50 and at that time, the commercial area will increase to 25% of the total homepage for all offices in GeGa Weekly Inc. The representatives of IKEA and IMEI will update their own homepages. When the number of branch offices is more than 1000, the commercial space will increase to 33% of the total homepage for all offices in GeGa Weekly.

Partners:

The starting partners will be Commonwealth Magazine (CM), IKEA, IMEI and Seattle virtuous-Events and wonderful-Arts Association（SEAA）SEAA will provide 0.1% or 1% of initial fund and each of CM, IKEA and IMEI will provide 33.3% or 33% of the initial fund, the percentage will be decided.

There will be seven workers when GeGa Weekly starts. Four of them will come from retired workers of CM: one CEO, one Logistic Manager, one Chief Editor and one IT Manager. IKEA and IMEI should assign a contact worker from their Public Relation (PR) departments to handle the free 1/10 space at the main homepage of GeGa Weekly.

SEAA will be the coordinator 連絡人 and the worker to establish the Seattle branch in the future. The wage system as well as how to distribute profits are all written in the charter. The stockowners will vote to change the charter based on the percentages of their holding stocks. Here is a draft of the charter.

A draft of the charter:

This draft of the charter for GeGa Weekly will be finalized by the board members and be voted in the meeting of all stockholders.

1. The definition of practical news, will be voted by the ongoing board members and the board members will be elected by the meeting of all stockholders.
2. The wage system is very simple, frontline workers will be paid average wage and benefits of same kind job at related local areas. A lead worker is a frontline worker who also provide on-job training to other frontline workers. If there is a lead worker, the lead worker will receive 110% of the average wage and benefits from all frontline workers under the lead worker. All the managers are paid by wage as well. A manager receives the average wage and benefits of all workers directly report to that manager. Yes, so simple; everyone is paid by wage and overtime is available for everyone to help adopting changes.
3. The distribution of profits is also very simple, most of the profits go to open new branch offices. In the first five years, no more than 5% of profits should go to investors; in the second five years, no more than 10% of profits should go to investors and after that no more than 15% of profits should go to investors.

How to start GeGa Weekly?

Procedure 1: SEAA needs to talk to the Commonwealth Magazine (CM) first. If CM and SEAA can reach some agreement then CM and SEAA will contact IKEA and IMEI for their input regarding the initial investment amount. If CM and SEAA should find another investors to replace IKEA or IMEI, CM may provide a list of potential businesses to invite.

Procedure 2: After investors are ready, GeGa Weekly may rent an office space within CM and CM will assign four retired workers as board members of GeGa Weekly to work with me to draft the charter.

Procedure 3: The next step is the draft of charter should be presented to the stockholders' meeting for approval. After that, the first version of the definition of practical/useful news will be decided by the board members.

After that, the IT Manager will try to design the homepage, the CEO and Chief Editor will try to collect sources of news, the Logistic Manager will prepare the hardware of the rented office and SEAA will coordinate with all of them regarding how to organize the practical news all over the world on the website so that people will like to visit the website continuously. Subscribers can also order paper version of GeGa Weekly.

Procedure 4: The next step is the CEO will call IKEA and IMEI for their input about the homepage. The Chief Editor and SEAA will start to group some news in last year and last month together as samples to attract potential customers of paid commercials.

To report practical/useful good news truly and interestingly is the ongoing key issue to attract subscribers and commercial customers.

If it is possible, CM could open a branch offices in Seattle, USA to start the US branch at the same time.

Procedure 5: Then, CM will create a big icon at the homepage for GeGa Weekly after GeGa Weekly has received deposits for all of the 8/10 available commercial spaces at homepage. After that, GeGa Weekly is officially established.

Procedure 6: The next goal is to create American branch office if not started yet and SEAA will work on it. At that time, or, 2 years later, if the American branch already opened with Taiwan headquarters, the summary will come with pronunciation.

Tiny APA fonts will be put beneath each word of the summaries. This will be a big jump of GeGa Weekly, people can use it as a tool of learning Chinese and English languages. The screen will allow split-windows so that same summary can be displayed by two windows, side by side, of different languages with APA to mark pronunciations of both languages. APA will be extended to cover all main languages. Currently APA can cover English, Chinese, Taiwanese, Hakka, Japanese, Korean and Spanish.

Then, if it is successful, GeGa Weekly will open three more branches, Hong Kong branch, Japan branch and Korea branch.

After the company is established like that, GeGa Weekly can try to sell itself to Google or other big international company and each GeGa Weekly offices will reduce to branch offices of GeWeekly (Google Events Weekly Inc. 谷歌事件周刊) or XeWeekly and CM can be one of three starting partners. ET could occupy the center 1/10 space for educational businesses on the homepage of GeWeekly or XeWeekly if ET wishes to do so.

Three Steps:

The first step is in Traditional Chinese with optional translation to Simplified Chinese and American English only. This is when GeGaWI has offices in Taiwan only.

The second step starts with the American branch office or two years later if American branch already opened, each summary will come with APA to mark each word of the summaries. GeGaWI will change logo to include its Chinese name.

The third step will start after APA is accepted and the APA for Hong Kong, Japan and Korea is ready to go. GeGaWI will open three more branches. Then, try to sell itself to Google or some international company.

8-7. Baha'u'llhism
勤教

I hope there exist a belief which is able to bridge the religious people and non-religious people.

My suggestion is that we may select Baha'u'llah of Baha'i Faith as the Saint of the belief and name the belief as Baha'u'llhism. The believers of Baha'u'llhism is named Baha'u'llhists.

A Baha'u'llhist believes in one Saint, Baha'u'llah; four religions and three believes. The four religions are Christianity, Islamism, Sikhism and Baha'i Faith and the three believes are Zen, Confucianism and Taoism.

The main teachings of the four religions are love everyone even your enemy, help people, all people are equal and same God respectively. The main teachings of the three believes are be merciful and hold on laws, be frugal and hold on true love and then be yielding and hold on logic respectively.

133

The main teaching of Baha'u'llhsim is be diligent.
勤教的主要教義是勤快。

Baha'u'llhsts believe in principle 132, P132, which is one bag of three gems and two self-controls.

The bag is "be diligent" and the gems in the bag are the three treasures of Laozi, "be merciful, frugal and yielding" while two self-controls are related to revenging and looking for a win-win solution.

There are two kinds of revenge, one is trying to live better than your foe/enemy and the other kind is trying to make your foe/enemy sorrowful. You like to control yourself to stay on the first kind.

My suggestion on the second self-control is that, don't start working on a win-win solution if your ability or the timing is not there yet. You like to wait for the right time while improving yourself.

8-8. Today
今天

What I say and do today decide my future and define me.

今日的言行造就明日的我。

My suggestion of the guideline for daily behaviors is P132. It was explained in detail on page 66 of "Special Relativity of Roses & Happiness".

我認為人們的言行規範可以簡化為 P132。在 "玫瑰和幸福的狹義相對論" 第 66 頁我已經把它詳細說明了一次。

Phonetic Table

B (Bopomofo), P (Pinyin), A (APA), 白（白話字）

B	ㄅ	ㄆ	ㄇ	ㄈ	ㄉ	ㄊ	ㄋ	ㄌ	ㄍ	ㄎ	ㄏ	(ㄐ	ㄑ	ㄒ)
P	b	p	m	f	d	t	n	l	g	k	h	(j	q	x)
A	b	p	m	f	d	t	n	l	g	k	h	(ds	ts	s)
白	p	ph	m		t	th	n	l	k	kh	h	(chi	chhi	si)

B	ㄓ	ㄔ	ㄕ	ㄖ	ㄗ	ㄘ	ㄙ				ㄚ	ㄛ	ㄜ	ㄝ
P	zh	ch	sh	r	z	c	s				a	o	e	e
A	dR	tR	sR	R	ds	ts	s	B	G	N	a	o	E	e
白					ch	chh	s	b	g	n	a	o	o	e

B	ㄞ	ㄟ	ㄠ	ㄡ	(ㄢ)	ㄣ	(ㄤ)	ㄥ	ㄦ	ㄧ	ㄨ	ㄩ
P	ai	ei	ao	ou	(an)	n	(ang)	ng	er	y i	w u	ü
A	ai	ei	au	ou	(an)	n	(ang)	ng	ER	y i	w u	yu
白	ai		au		(an)	n	(ang)	ng		i	o u	oa oe ui

English word:	cup	hit	book	cat	very	red	zoo	you
Key letter	u	i	oo	a	v	r	z	you
APA letter	A	I	U	ae	v	r	z	iu
白 letter							z	iu

English word:	judge	church	ship	vision	this	thin
Key letter	j	ch	sh	s	th	th
APA letter	dZ	tZ	sZ	Z	D	T

* Tone marks

	1	2	3	4	5	6	7	
Bopomofo		/	v	\	.			
Pinyin	-	/	v	\				
APA	^	/	v	\	-	v-	>	
白		/	v	\		^	-	.
白（調號）	2	4	6	3	1	5	7	8
pitch level	Mi	ReMi	Do	MiDo	Do#	DoDo#	Re	Re
active mood	So	MiSo	Do	SoDo	Re	DoRe	Mi	Mi

138

What I say and do today
wat   ai   sei   aend   du   tU-dei\

decide my future
dI-sai^d   mai   fyu^tZEr

and define me.
aend   dI-fain^   mi

今 日 的 言 行
dsin^   R\   dE-   yen/   sing/

造 就 明 日 的 我 。
dsau\   dsyou\   ming/   R\   dE-   wov

我 今 仔 日 所 講 所 做 的 啊 若
Gwa- gin- a^ zi- so^ gong\ so^ dsEv ev mv nav

決 定 我 的 將 來 也 同 時
gwad^dingvGwa- e- dsyong-lai/ yav dong- si/

記 錄 我 的 靈 魂 。
gi\ lov Gwa- e- ling- hwn/

The dewdrop at each tip of grass leaves
is like the perfect job for each
mind of willing workers.

-     A Taiwanese Proverb

一枝草，一點露；
用心找就有頭路。

-     台灣諺語